SHAKESPEARE FOR EVERYONE

AS YOU LIKE IT

By Jennifer Mulherin *Illustrations by* George Thompson

PETER BEDRICK BOOKS
NEW YORK

Author's note

There is no substitute for seeing the plays of Shakespeare performed. Only then can you really understand why Shakespeare is our greatest dramatist and poet. This book simply gives you the background to the play and tells you about the story and characters. It will, I hope, encourage you to see the play.

Published by
Peter Bedrick Books
2112 Broadway
New York, NY 10023

Library of Congress Cataloguing in Publication Data

Mulherin, Jennifer.
    As you like it/by Jennifer Mulherin: illustrations by George
Thompson
    p. cm. – (Shakespeare for everyone)
    Summary: Discusses the plot, characters, and historical background
of the Shakespeare play.
    ISBN 0-87226-339-8
    1. Shakespeare, William, 1564-1616. As you like it – Juvenile
literature. [1. Shakespeare, William, 1564-1616. As you like it.
2. English literature – History and criticism.] I. Thompson,
George, 1944- ill. II. Title. III. Series: Mulherin, Jennifer.
Shakespeare for everyone.
PR2803.M8 1990   90-478
822.3′3–dc20   CIP
                                                    AC

Printed in Hong Kong

5 4 3 2 1 90 91 92 93 94 95

Contents

As You Like It *and Elizabethan country life*

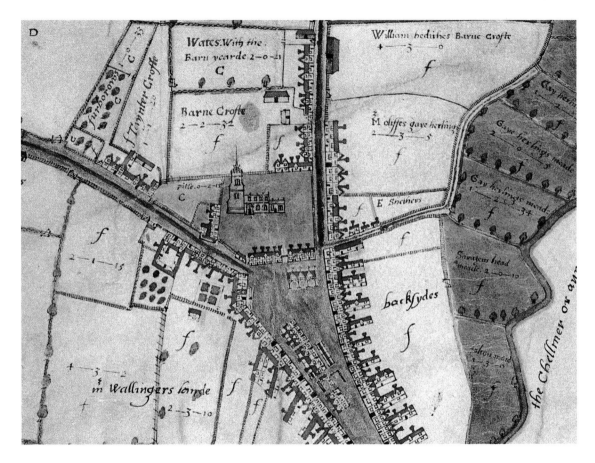

This detail from a map of Chelmsford, Essex, in 1591 shows the layout of a country town. Note the houses along the main street and the church with tower on the green.

Just as today, city people in Elizabethan times thought that life in the country was carefree and simple. Shakespeare supported this rosy view in *As You Like It*. In the Forest of Arden, all problems are solved and everyone achieves happiness. The truth about Elizabethan country life was different. For most people it was a hard life but one that fortunately had its compensations.

How the land was used

In Elizabethan times, the land was used to grow crops and also as pasture for animals. How the land was divided up differed from area to area. In some parts of England, pasture land was more popular than arable land. Sheep farming was very profitable in the early part of the 16th century, so many landowners stopped growing crops in order to graze sheep. It only takes one shepherd to look after a flock of sheep. It takes many hands to plough, sow and harvest a crop. So when farmers turned to sheep, many farm workers lost their jobs. Some became vagabonds who roamed the country looking for work. Others went to the cities to seek their fortune.

In Warwickshire, where Shakespeare spent his youth, the land was divided into two almost equal parts. To the south of the river Avon, there were fields of crops such as rye, wheat, corn and barley. To the north, in the forest of Arden, the land was used for grazing sheep and cattle. So shepherds like Corin and goatherds like Audrey, who appear in the play, really did exist in the forest that Shakespeare was writing about.

This illustration is from Shepherd's Calendar *by Sir Edmund Spenser. It depicts two shepherds with their flocks in the month of July.*

4

Haymaking in the early 17th century. Both women and children helped in the fields when a family was too poor to hire labourers.

With 1 shilling = 12 pence, 25 shillings equalled 300 pence, which would buy 100 chickens at 3 pence each. If today a chicken costs $5 then a shepherd in Elizabethan times earned in a year the equivalent of $1500.00.

Country labourers

Corin in *As You Like It* describes himself as 'a true labourer'. He says, 'I earn that I eat, get that I wear, owe no man hate, envy no man's happiness.' He had to be content with small wages. Shepherds were usually hired by owners of country estates for a year at a time. They received between 25 and 30 shillings for their year's work but their food and lodgings were free. Other workers were paid by the day and worked for a number of masters. Harvesters, for instance, could earn between threepence and sevenpence a day and thatchers were quite well paid at two shillings for five days. In the seasons when such people could not find work for their skills, they might work as farm helpers, doing odd jobs. For this type of work, they were paid one or two pence a day. In those days, a chicken cost about threepence and beer one penny a gallon.

Ordinary country folk worked long hours all the year round and in all weathers. They had few of the comforts of life and were rarely able to save much from what they earned.

Poor but honest farmers

The master and mistress of a small country farm may have employed some labourers part-time. But they worked just as hard as any of their hired help. The farmer and his family lived in a small thatched cottage and everyone in the household helped with daily tasks. The farmer himself worked long hours in the field, yoking his oxen and tending his pigs. His wife did the household chores, sometimes with the help of a maid. She was also expected to brew ale, attend to the dairy and look after the chickens and ducks. It was her task, too, to ride to market and sell butter, cheese, eggs, chickens and whatever else the farm produced.

Anne Hathaway's cottage at Shottery near Stratford-upon-Avon. This thatched-roofed country dwelling belonged to the family of Shakespeare's wife, who were farmers. It still stands today.

A country woman taking her poultry to market. Women often walked several miles to the nearest town to sell their produce.

A small farmer never became very rich but his family was rarely short of food; they produced it all themselves. Like most country people, they were generous to the poor and took pity on vagabonds and others who had fallen on hard times. They gave them food and sometimes shelter. They knew that, but for good fortune, they could be in the same position.

Country amusements

Although country people did not have much leisure, there were village festivals and feastdays when they could have fun. Harvest time, for example, was a time for celebration. After the last sheaf of corn was carried through the village in a procession, everyone joined in a banquet. As well as eating, there was much dancing, drinking and singing. This was a great occasion, too, for young people to flirt and dance with

7

This illustration depicts a country festival. The celebration of May Day and other feastdays and festivals were important events in Elizabethan country life. They provided an opportunity for dancing, merrymaking and feasting.

each other. Sweethearts exchanged gloves or handkerchiefs as keepsakes.

Another happy event in out-of-the-way country districts was the visit of the pedlar. He was a travelling salesman who carried all sorts of wonderful treasures from the outside world. Pots and pans, toys, ribbons, silks and gloves were just some of the items he sold. The entire village and even the lords and ladies in the manor house came out to buy his goods. Young women, particularly, loved to spend their hard-earned money on the pretty finery he carried. Many milkmaids, for instance, were known to squander more than half their wages with the pedlar.

A hard but happy life?

Although country life was physically exhausting in Elizabethan times, few country dwellers were discontented. If they had a few acres to till or regular work from an honest master, they felt secure. They did not envy merchants or townspeople. They scarcely knew how they lived and cared less. Most of them thanked God for what they had and did not desire more.

A rural setting

This 19th-century painting shows a scene from As You Like It. *Orlando has accepted a challenge from the champion wrestler, Charles. Rosalind and Celia are clearly concerned for his life.*

Most of *As You Like It* is set in the countryside. Books and poems about the imaginary life of shepherds and milkmaids were very fashionable in Shakespeare's day. Two writers before Shakespeare had written pastoral 'romances' – Edmund Spenser in *Shepherd's Calendar* (1579) and Sir Philip Sidney in *Arcadia* (1590). Shakespeare's audience at the Globe Theatre was, therefore, already familiar with stories about happy country life. And, as city folk who rarely had a chance to visit the country, they liked them.

Shakespeare's story

Shakespeare borrowed his story from a romance by Thomas Lodge called *Rosalynde*, which was published in 1590. This was a popular work which had been reprinted many times. As in Shakespeare's play, the main character is a young girl and most of the action is set in a forest. But in *As You Like It* Shakespeare invented new characters, such as Jaques, Audrey and Touchstone, and left out many scenes, particularly battles, that were in Lodge's story.

In Lodge's romance, the characters are elegant, clever people. They are more like courtiers than country folk. Shakespeare's characters are more realistic. Corin, Audrey and William are real country people. So, although Shakespeare used Lodge's story, he made it different and improved on it.

When the play was written

As You Like It was probably written in 1599, the year in which the Globe Theatre opened. It could not have been written before 1598 because Phebe, the shepherdess, quotes some lines from the poem *Hero and Leander* by Shakespeare's friend, Christopher Marlowe. This poem was only published in 1598.

Scholars also think that Jaques's famous speech 'All the world's a stage' may have been written to celebrate the opening of the Globe Theatre. Others say the play was privately performed at the wedding of Shakespeare's patron, the Earl of Southampton, in 1598; this would account for the appearance of the god of marriage at the end of the play.

The Forest of Arden

In Lodge's *Rosalynde*, the forest is in the Ardennes, a region in northeastern France. Shakespeare seemed to be thinking of this setting when he gave many of his characters French

An Elizabethan shepherdess, complete with a fashionable ruff. Finery like this, which was often worn by town and city ladies, was usually bought from travelling pedlars.

An 18th-century depiction of the wrestling scene in As You Like It *. Here, the characters are in 18th-century clothes, not in Elizabethan dress.*

names. But Shakespeare's forest is more like the Arden district of Warwickshire where he grew up. The ordinary country characters in the play are probably similar to people he knew as a boy.

Shakespeare's forest is not entirely realistic. Although sheep and deer live in it, they have exotic olives and palms to browse on, trees not usually found in English forests. The old Duke proclaims that the only dangers in the forest are winter and foul weather - though, as the audience learns, there are also green and gold snakes – and the occasional lion.

In the play, the forest is a special place to which people escape from the harshness of the world. Once there, the characters seem to forget their troubles. Like the banished

Duke and his followers, they 'fleet the time carelessly as they did in the golden world'. Even the wicked characters find peace and happiness in the Forest of Arden. It changes Oliver and Duke Frederick, for example, from their evil ways into good men. Although real country people live in it, the forest changes outsiders into contented people. Shakespeare really does make it a 'golden world'.

Shakespeare's language

When *As You Like It* is performed on the stage, it is easier to understand than many of his other plays. This is because a great deal of it is written in conversational prose rather than verse. Before Shakespeare's time, most playwrights wrote in verse with strict rhyme and rhythms that were rather stilted. Shakespeare was following a current fashion when many of the comedies presented at court were written in a form of stylish prose. In this play, ordinary people like Touchstone and Audrey almost always speak everyday language. The other characters use a mixture of prose and verse. When Shakespeare wants his characters to say something important or with great feeling, they usually speak verse. 'All the world's a stage', for example, is in verse but Rosalind's and Orlando's love game is spoken in prose. The 'conversation' in *As You Like It* helps to make the characters more life-like.

Written in a hurry?

Some scholars suggest this play was written in a hurry. They mention the title of the play, suggesting that Shakespeare had no time to think of a proper title. They say there is not much of a story, and that the scenes with songs are there to cover this up. Shakespeare has two characters in the play called Jaques, which is not particularly confusing, but was probably an oversight on his part. He also gives contradictory descriptions of the height of Rosalind and

The Elizabethans believed that the toad had a precious jewel in its head which was an antidote to poison. The old Duke refers to this superstition in the play. He compares the hardships of life in the forest to the ugly toad, but points out that there is 'good in every thing'.

A nobleman and his lady in Shakespeare's time. Shakespeare was familiar with court life, which he describes in this play, through his patron, the Earl of Southampton.

Celia. Shakespeare often made a few mistakes like this, sometimes because he was revising a play for a different audience or for different actors. This did not worry the Elizabethan audiences who were used to different versions of the same play. They were also used to the same play with a different title. 'As you like it' could mean 'call it what you want'.

Shakespeare's titles

Shakespeare always had a rather casual attitude to titles. His play *Twelfth Night* has no obvious connection to the post-Christmas festival and is subtitled 'What You Will'. Another comedy is called *Much Ado About Nothing*. Titles clearly were not of great importance. Probably, as today, the playwright's name was all that was needed to attract an audience.

13

The story of
As You Like It

Orlando is badly treated by his elder brother, Oliver. He tells Adam, their dead father's old servant, that Oliver will not give him the money left to him by their father. Instead, he makes him work like a poor peasant.

Oliver plots against his brother
Oliver and Orlando quarrel and Oliver decides on revenge against his brother. He arranges a wrestling match between the champion, Charles, and his brother. Charles is instructed to kill Orlando.

The banished Duke
Meanwhile at court, the old Duke has been banished by his younger brother, Duke Frederick, who now rules the land. The old Duke and his followers have fled to the Forest of Arden where they live in peace and harmony. Rosalind is the old Duke's daughter but she has been allowed to stay at court because she is the greatest friend of Celia, Duke Frederick's daughter.

The wrestling match
The court has gathered to watch the wrestling match between Orlando and Charles. Rosalind has fallen in love with Orlando at first sight and she begs him not to fight. Orlando insists, saying it does not matter if he dies.

Orlando before the wrestling match
I shall do my friends no wrong, for I have none to lament me; the world no injury, for in it I have nothing . . .

Act I Sc ii

In fact, Orlando throws Charles and wins the wrestling match. Rosalind is delighted and gives him a locket. When

15

Duke Frederick learns that Orlando is the son of an enemy, he is displeased and he dismisses him.

Rosalind is banished

Rosalind confesses to Celia that she has fallen in love with Orlando. They are disturbed by Celia's father who angrily accuses Rosalind of being a traitor. He orders her to leave the kingdom. Celia asks the Duke for a reason but he merely points out how much people admire Rosalind.

Why Rosalind must leave

She is too subtle for thee; and her smoothness,
Her very silence and her patience,
Speak to the people, and they pity her.
Thou art a fool: she robs thee of thy name . . .

Act I Sc iii

Celia declares she will go into exile with Rosalind. The two decide to seek out Rosalind's father in the Forest of Arden. Disguised as a young man called Ganymede, Rosalind will accompany a 'sister', Celia. Touchstone, the court jester, agrees to go with them.

Meanwhile, in the Forest of Arden, the old Duke and his followers muse on how pleasant their simple life is compared to that at court.

The pleasures of country life

And this our life exempt from public haunt,
Finds tongues in trees, books in the running brooks,
Sermons in stones, and good in every thing.

Act II Sc i

Back at Oliver's house, Orlando learns from Adam that his brother plans another attempt on his life. He decides to flee, and Adam begs to go with him. When Adam offers Orlando all his money, the young man is touched. Together, they go off to seek their fortune.

> **Orlando expresses his gratitude**
> *O good old man! how well in thee appears*
> *The constant service of the antique world,*
> *When service sweat for duty, not for meed!*
>
> Act II Sc iii

In the Forest of Arden

Celia, Rosalind and Touchstone at last arrive in the Forest of Arden. They are so weary they can go no further. By chance, they overhear a young shepherd, Silvius, talking to an older man, Corin, about his love for a shepherdess called Phebe. They ask Corin where they can get food and shelter. He leads them to a sheep farm which is for sale. They like it and decide to buy it.

At the old Duke's encampment

Orlando and Adam arrive in the Forest of Arden but Adam is too weak from hunger to go on. Orlando goes in search of food. Meanwhile, the Duke's followers are singing a song.

A country song

Under the greenwood tree
Who loves to lie with me,
And turn his merry note
Unto the sweet bird's throat.

Act II Sc v

Orlando comes upon the Duke's encampment. He threatens to kill everyone unless he is given food. The Duke answers him politely and offers his hospitality. Orlando apologises for being rude and goes to fetch Adam. Jaques, a melancholy nobleman, talks about the life of man. He says it is rather like a stage play with seven different acts.

Seven ages of man

All the world's a stage,
And all the men and women merely players:
They have their exits and their entrances;
And one man in his time plays many parts,
His acts being seven ages. At first the infant,
Mewling and puking in the nurse's arms ...
...And then the lover,
Sighing like furnace, with a woful ballad
Made to his mistress' eyebrow ... Last scene of all,
That ends this strange eventful history,
Is second childishness and mere oblivion,
Sans teeth, sans eyes, sans taste, sans everything.

Act II Sc vii

18

The second age of man

And then the whining school-boy,
with his satchel,
And shining morning face,
creeping like snail
Unwillingly to school . . .

Back at court, Duke Frederick questions Oliver about his brother's disappearance. He orders him to find Orlando and bring him back, dead or alive.

In praise of Rosalind

Orlando hangs verses in praise of Rosalind on trees in the forest. They are found by both Rosalind and Celia. Celia, who has seen Orlando in the forest, reveals that the verses are his. Just as Rosalind is eagerly questioning her friend, Orlando arrives. Rosalind, dressed as Ganymede, approaches him. She talks to him about love and offers to cure his lovesickness by pretending to be his Rosalind – whom he must woo.

Rosalind's views on love

Love is merely a madness, and, I tell you, deserves as well a dark house and a whip as madmen do.

Act III Sc ii

Orlando does not want to be cured of love but he likes talking to Ganymede. He agrees to take her cure.

The jester in love

Meanwhile, Touchstone has fallen in love with Audrey, a simple country girl who tends goats. He has arranged to be married to her by a local vicar in the forest. Jaques, who has overheard their talk, tells Touchstone to get married properly in a church.

'The proud disdainful shepherdess'

Silvius, the young shepherd, is having no luck in winning the love of Phebe. Celia and Rosalind watch unnoticed as she scorns his love in a cruel way. Rosalind steps forward and rebukes Phebe for rejecting Silvius.

The wooing of Rosalind

As arranged, Orlando visits Rosalind for his love 'cure'.
'Come, woo me, woo me; for now I am in a holiday humour,
and like enough to consent,' she says. Orlando says he would
die for love of Rosalind but 'Ganymede' scoffs at this
romantic idea.

> ## To die for love?
> *. . . men have died from time to time, and worms have eaten them, but not for love.*
>
> Act IV Sc i

Orlando soon has to hurry away to keep an appointment. Rosalind eagerly awaits his return in a couple of hours.

Meanwhile, Silvius delivers a letter from Phebe to Rosalind. He is unaware of its contents but Phebe has fallen in love with 'Ganymede'. It is a love letter.

Enter Oliver

Just then Oliver arrives looking for Celia and Rosalind. He tells that he was sleeping in the forest and that a lioness was ready to pounce on him. He was rescued by Orlando but in the struggle Orlando was wounded by the beast. Overcome with gratitude and love, Oliver tells how he has become reunited with his brother.

He carries Orlando's bloodstained handkerchief, and a message for the youth 'Rosalind' – Orlando cannot keep his appointment. So alarming is this news that Rosalind faints, but she quickly pretends she is only play-acting. She is weak and pale, though, and has to be helped back to the cottage.

Audrey's suitor dismissed

Audrey complains to Touchstone about not being married yet. He asks her to be patient. Just then, a young country boy, William, arrives. He is interested in courting Audrey. Touchstone talks to him, showing off his clever, courtly ways. He threatens him and then sends him on his way in no uncertain terms.

22

Love at first sight

Oliver tells Orlando that he and Celia have fallen in love and intend to marry. He bequeaths his inheritance to Orlando, declaring that he intends to lead the life of a shepherd in the forest. Orlando and Rosalind discuss the good news. She explains that it was love at first sight.

Orlando wishes that he too could be married to his Rosalind. Rosalind reveals that she has magic powers and can make this happen. Phebe and Silvius arrive. Although he is still in love with Phebe, she wants to marry Ganymede. Rosalind promises that all their wishes will be fulfilled the following day.

What love is
It is to be all made of fantasy,
All made of passion, and all made of wishes;
All adoration, duty and observance;
All humbleness, all patience, and impatience;
All purity, all trial, all obeisance.

Act v Sc ii

A joyful day
Touchstone and Audrey too are looking forward to the following day when they are to be married. Two of the Duke's pages sing them a charming love song.

Rosalind's promises
On the day when Rosalind's promises are to be fulfilled, she explains to the old Duke exactly what they are. If his daughter, Rosalind, appears she will be given in marriage to Orlando. The Duke agrees to this, as does Orlando. Phebe promises that she will marry Ganymede – but, if she changes her mind, she agrees to marry Silvius. Celia and Rosalind then leave to prepare for the celebrations.

Touchstone and Audrey arrive. Jaques recognizes him as the jester he has often seen in the forest. Having spoken to Touchstone, he knows that the jester has lived at court. Touchstone amuses the company with his talk of how a

24

A love song
It was a lover and his lass,
*   With a hey, and a ho, and a hey nonino,*
That o'er the green corn-field did pass,
*   In the spring time, the only pretty ring time,*
When birds do sing, hey ding a ding, ding;
Sweet lovers love the spring.

Act v Sc ii

courtier behaves. He asks if he and Audrey can be married with the other couples.

> **The courtier, Touchstone**
> *... I have trod a measure; I have flattered a lady; I have been politic with my friend, smooth with mine enemy; I have undone three tailors ...*
>
> Act v Sc iv

Celia and Rosalind arrive dressed in court clothes. The god of marriage arrives to bestow a solemn blessing on the couples.

The promises fulfilled

All the puzzles are now solved. Orlando realises that the young man he has wooed is his beloved Rosalind. Phebe now knows that Ganymede is a girl and agrees to marry Silvius.

Just then Jaques, the youngest brother of Orlando and Oliver, arrives with important news. Celia's father, who had set out to confront the old Duke in the forest, has been converted to a religious life. He met a hermit on the way and has given his crown and lands to the old Duke. The melancholy Jaques, who believes that he can learn much by taking up a religious life, decides to join Duke Frederick. The rest of the company prepare to celebrate the young couples' marriages.

Rosalind's epilogue

The play is over and Rosalind comes on to the stage to talk to the audience. She jokes with them, saying that a good play should not need an epilogue. She asks the men and women in turn to approve of the play. She then curtsies and bids the audience farewell.

27

The play's characters

Rosalind

Orlando

Rosalind in love

... I will be more jealous of thee than a Barbary cock-pigeon over his hen; more clamorous than a parrot against rain; more new-fangled than an ape; more giddy in my desires than a monkey ...

Act IV Sc i

Rosalind
Rosalind is one of the most charming of all Shakespeare's female characters. She is bright, witty and able to talk and joke with everyone. She is at her most attractive in the wooing game she plays with Orlando. Although she flirts with him, she also talks a lot of common sense. Even though she is dressed as a boy, she behaves with girlish feelings. She faints, for instance, when she hears that Orlando has been wounded. She has, however, to use her imagination to solve the problems created by her Ganymede identity.

Orlando
Brave, strong and handsome, Orlando seems a worthy lover for any young woman. He has a generous, kind nature which shows in the care he takes of Adam. Although he has been badly treated by his brother, he nobly rescues him from the lioness. He is a true gentleman despite his life as a peasant; he apologises to the gentle Duke for his impolite behaviour. His verses to Rosalind show him to be romantic. However, in the wooing game with Rosalind, she does seem to outtalk him with her witty comments.

Celia

Celia is Rosalind's dearest friend and the two girls are as close as sisters. Celia's great quality is her loyalty to her friend. When Rosalind is banished by Duke Frederick, Celia chooses to go with her. This is not only because she loves her friend but also because she believes her father is wrong in calling Rosalind a traitor. Like Rosalind, she is witty and amusing. She teases Rosalind about being in love with Orlando and about his verses. Although she warns Rosalind against love at first sight, she falls instantly in love with Oliver. Her warm and generous nature make her very appealing and the audience knows that she will make the perfect wife – even as a shepherdess.

Oliver

At the beginning of the play, Oliver is a villain. Not only does he treat his brother with contempt, he also wants to kill him. He is jealous of Orlando's good nature and popularity. When the wrestler fails to kill Orlando as planned, Oliver makes another attempt. It is hard to believe that such a character can have a complete change of heart, but he does. After his rescue by Orlando, his good qualities emerge.

A close friendship

. . . we still have slept together,
Rose at an instant, learn'd, play'd, eat together;
And whereso'er we went, like Juno's swans,
Still we went coupled and inseparable.

Act I Sc iii

Oliver

Celia

Oliver's nature

O! I have heard him speak of that same brother;
And he did render him the most unnatural
That liv'd 'mongst men.

Act IV Sc iii

29

A fool's life

He uses his folly like a stalking-horse, and
under the presentation of that he shoots his wit.

Act v Sc iv

Jaques

Audrey

Touchstone

Melancholy Jaques

... it is a melancholy of mine own, compounded of
many simples, extracted from many objects, and
indeed the sundry contemplation of my travels,
which, by often rumination, wraps me in a most
humorous sadness.

Act iv Sc i

Jaques

Jaques is one of the old Duke's followers. He is a melancholy person who is always thinking and talking about the meaning of life. When a deer is slaughtered he weeps in sympathy with the animal. He sees a moral in almost everything that happens. And he is also clever and wise about the ways of the world. In the play his main purpose is to comment on the actions of the other characters.

Touchstone

Touchstone is a court jester. He earns his living by playing the fool and amusing people. He makes fun of Orlando's love verses and jokes about country ways and court manners. He brings people down to earth with his clever comments. He marries Audrey but unlike the other lovers, he hopes to get out of it afterwards.

Audrey

Audrey is an ordinary country girl who looks after goats. She is not very clever but she has an honest, simple nature which is why Touchstone likes her. And she is probably flattered to find favour with such a worldly man. She is not a make-believe country person, but a real one.

The life and plays of Shakespeare

Life of Shakespeare

1564 William Shakespeare born at Stratford-upon-Avon.

1582 Shakespeare marries Anne Hathaway, eight years his senior.

1583 Shakespeare's daughter, Susanna, is born.

1585 The twins, Hamnet and Judith, are born.

1587 Shakespeare goes to London.

1591-2 Shakespeare writes *The Comedy of Errors*. He is becoming well-known as an actor and writer.

1592 Theatres closed because of plague.

1593-4 Shakespeare writes *Titus Andronicus* and *The Taming of the Shrew*: he is member of the theatrical company, the Chamberlain's Men.

1594-5 Shakespeare writes *Romeo and Juliet*.

1595 Shakespeare writes *A Midsummer Night's Dream*.

1595-6 Shakespeare writes *Richard II*.

1596 Shakespeare's son, Hamnet, dies. He writes *King John* and *The Merchant of Venice*.

1597 Shakespeare buys New Place in Stratford.

1597-8 Shakespeare writes *Henry IV*.

1599 Shakespeare's theatre company opens the Globe Theatre.

1599-1600 Shakespeare writes *As You Like It*, *Henry V* and *Twelfth Night*.

1600-01 Shakespeare writes *Hamlet*.

1602-03 Shakespeare writes *All's Well That Ends Well*.

1603 Elizabeth I dies. James I becomes king. Theatres closed because of plague.

1603-04 Shakespeare writes *Othello*.

1605 Theatres closed because of plague.

1605-06 Shakespeare writes *Macbeth* and *King Lear*.

1606-07 Shakespeare writes *Antony and Cleopatra*.

1607 Susanna Shakespeare marries Dr John Hall. Theatres closed because of plague.

1608 Shakespeare's granddaughter, Elizabeth Hall, is born.

1609 *Sonnets* published. Theatres closed because of plague.

1610 Theatres closed because of plague. Shakespeare gives up his London lodgings and retires to Stratford.

1611-12 Shakespeare writes *The Tempest*.

1613 Globe Theatre burns to the ground during a performance of Henry VIII.

1616 Shakespeare dies on 23 April.

Shakespeare's plays

The Comedy of Errors
Love's Labour's Lost
Henry VI Part 2
Henry VI Part 3
Henry VI Part 1
Richard III
Titus Andronicus
The Taming of the Shrew
The Two Gentlemen of Verona
Romeo and Juliet
Richard II
A Midsummer Night's Dream
King John
The Merchant of Venice
Henry IV Part 1
Henry IV Part 2
Much Ado About Nothing
Henry V
Julius Caesar
As You Like It
Twelfth Night
Hamlet
The Merry Wives of Windsor
Troilus and Cressida
All's Well That Ends Well
Othello
Measure for Measure
King Lear
Macbeth
Antony and Cleopatra
Timon of Athens
Coriolanus
Pericles
Cymbeline
The Winter's Tale
The Tempest
Henry VIII

Index

Numerals in *italics* refer to picture captions.

Acknowledgements
The publishers would like to thank Jenny Marshall for her help in producing this book.

Picture credits
p.1 Governors of Royal Shakespeare Theatre, Stratford-upon-Avon, p.3 reproduced by courtesy of Essex Record Office, p.9 Bridgeman Art Library, p.11 Tate Gallery.